BIBLE FORGET-ME-NOTS

MEMORY BOOK ONE

N. A. Woychuk, M.A., Th.D

Author "Messiah—A New Look at the Composer, the Music and the Message," "You Need to Memorize Scripture," "ABC Memory Book" and forty-five other memory books for all age levels, numerous other books and Bible games.

Cover and all illustrations, Mary Elizabeth Jones

Copyright © 1998 N. A. Woychuk, world rights reserved.

ISBN 1-880960-31-1 • Library of Congress Catalog Number 98-090493

New King James Version: Scriptures from the New King James Version © 1982. Thomas Nelson, Inc. Publishers. Used by permission. All rights reserved.

Scripture Memory Fellowship International

P. O. Box 411551 • St. Louis, MO 63141 • 314-569-0244

Printed in Korea

Acknowledgments

The name—Bible Forget-Me-Nots—comes from a little book for adults published in Boston exactly one hundred years ago, which I found in Oklahoma City.

Deep appreciation is expressed to all who have prayed for the development and the printing of this book and to all who have helped, particularly Sylvia Dorham, Jennifer Lamp, Betty Geer and Jim Woychuk.

Care has been taken to trace the ownership of every currently copyrighted selection included in this book and make full acknowledgment of its use. Any errors or omissions are unintentional and will be corrected in future editions. The publisher acknowledges with thanks permission received from the following to include the poems in this book:

Harcourt, Brace and Co., Inc. for "When Young Melissa Sweeps" from Magpie Lane, by Nancy Byrd Turner, copyright 1927 by Harcourt, Brace and Company, Inc., renewed 1955 by Nancy Byrd Turner; "Questions at Night" from Rainbow in the Sky, by Louis Untermeyer, copyright 1935 by Harcourt, Brace and Company, Inc. Western Publishing Co., Inc. for "God Watches Us" by Gabriel Setoun, "A Childs Prayer" by M. Betham Edwards, from *Prayers for Children*—A Little Golden Book; copyright 1942, 1952 by Western Publishing Company, Inc.

The Scope of This Memory Book

1. *The Infancy Connection*: Here is stated what God is teaching us about the memorizing of Scripture by infants from the very time of birth. Take time to read it.
2. Then come the ten Bible verses to be memorized, with the color illustrations and "little lights" which relate to the verses.
3. At the end of the book are the further illuminations on the Bible verses. Here you will find a reduced copy of the main color illustrations, a helpful commentary on the verses, a few songs and other items.

The Infancy Connection

In this amazing century of inventions, of technologies and of explorations, the most engrossing subject, in the estimation of many, is still the *brephos*, the *paidion*, the infant, the little child, and it will be the same a hundred years from now.

Let us consider if we are doing enough with those little ones.

> But what am I?
> An infant crying in the night:
> An infant crying for the light:
> And with no language but a cry.
> —Tennyson

The teaching of the child should begin before the "crying." Indeed, the old proverb has it that to train a child correctly you must begin with the grandmother. Increasingly scientists are confirming that biological and psychological traits are passed from generation to generation.

Physically the newborn comes fully equipped— "fearfully and wonderfully made" (Ps. 139:14). As an example, he "has all the muscles he will ever have, though they are small" (Enc. Britannica). Some authorities—beginning with *John Locke* (1632-1704)—tell us that cognitively the newborn "is a blank slate, a *tabula rasa.*" This is not acceptable. There is a growing body of evidence to suggest that the "slate" of a child in utero is being indelibly impressed. *Rene Van de Carr*, M. D. states, "Our own research and that of innumerable scientists in the field of prenatal development has shown that while inside the [womb] the baby is capable of learning, feeling, and telling the difference between dark and light."

Research also shows that "hearing is the first sense to develop in the unborn infant," and child specialists suggest that we speak softly and play soothing music and give the unborn child a sense of peace, well being and a developmental boost. Christian parents do well to begin quoting Scripture, and sing simple lyrics to the preborn child. When the baby arrives, he will already have begun to tuck away in his memory some of these eternal realities.

While unbelievers may attribute the child's developing characteristics to environment, we know that this beautiful baby comes with a sin nature (Ps. 51:5). *William Blake* put it gently when he wrote, "Sweet babe, in thy face soft desires I can trace, secret joys and secret smiles, little pretty infant wiles." In some mysterious way we "all have sinned" with Adam, our federal head (Rom. 3:23; 5:12). No child needs training in how to sin, and Satan is busy establishing his own connections in that little life and weaves a spiritual blindfold with respect to the great truth of redemption (2 Cor. 4:4). We give the Holy Spirit a solid foundation on which to counter Satan's efforts when we consistently feed the baby the word of God from her earliest days.

Unlike other creatures with basic instincts, the human infant comes utterly helpless; yet, "heaven lies about us in our infancy" (*Wordsworth*), and the extent of learning— mental and spiritual—is superior to all other creation because we are made "in the image of God," with eternity in our hearts.

The Experts

"Good Beginnings for All Children" was the name of a conference held in St. Louis, Missouri in 1997. It was attended by one hundred ten scientists and educational experts who delved into the development of children, birth to age three. *Carla Schatz*, professor of neurobiology at the University of California, Berkley, stated, "When babies are born, the wiring of the brain is not yet complete; experience can help influence the wiring of the brain."

The intended meaning of "experience" was not stated, but we may safely say the "influence" of godly parents, with words that weep, with tears that tell and with love that has no bounds is of all influences the most refined, the most creative, and will, at once, find the exact place in the brain of the child to form that needed *connection*.

It is at this point that the greatest authority on the children must be introduced.

Our dear Lord lifted the infant upon the highest plane for all time when He set the little child before the contentious apostles as a model of unconscious humility and of complete trustfulness (Matt. 18:1-5). The tiny creation, fresh from the immensities of the Infinite, evokes His fullest attention. He observes minutely the minds and the hearts of the infants. He sees all; He knows best; He understands every turn of their thoughts, their inclinations, their simple searching, their crying.

We quite naturally surround them with dolls, with bunnies, with rattles and with many toys, but they are capable of much more. Early there must come an effort to elicit from them some slight, beginning inclination to reach out to the blessed Savior. All who wait on these precious little bundles of life do well to regard themselves as the holy attendants of those who seem like little emigrants from the shores of Eternity and make it their chief concern to present them to the Lord of that Country, to surround them with sounds, with songs, with Scripture . . . and with love, with gentleness, with care and with that divine solicitude for their early attachment to the blessed Savior whose love yearns for them far beyond the love of any other. When you do this, you provide for them an inheritance far greater than any earthly treasure.

"From the Christian perspective, we need to remember that by the age of four a child has absorbed half of what will influence him the most the rest of his life" (*Jeanne Hendricks*).

Scientists like *Dr. Larry Katz*, neurobiologist at Duke University, tell us now that brains in children sprout when they are very young and continue "at a furious pace until they are about five years old." This rapid growth tapers off quickly "when new connections are no longer being made." Such conclusions should arouse Christian parents and educators.

Beginning Early

In Bible memorizing, let us determine to begin at the very earliest age possible. Let us not withhold the very best when the "windows of learning" are opening up. Put the little ones on the Word-bottle at the very beginning. For the last twelve days my daughter visited us with her little ten-month-old Allie; she was feeding her frequently throughout the day—from the time she awakened until she went to sleep. We must similarly feed our children the Word of God. The children will, of course, not register any spiritual responses, but their active little brains will be soaking it up, just as their growing bodies assimilate food. Remembering is an elusive process, but it is the glue of thinking. Their developing language is the remembering of the words most frequently spoken in their homes.

"Mother! father! watch and pray, fling not golden hours away!
Now or never, plant and sow, catch the morning's earliest glow."

Ideas in the mind of the infant first begin to be perceived by the senses. Light surprises; sound awakens. Emotions—in default of words—are the first unconscious language of the infant. Even the child whose senses are impaired is not caged in stillness and darkness. He begins to reach out for something beyond himself, just as naturally as the pale potato sprout in the dark cellar at our homestead in Sky Lake feebly reached for the light softly filtering inside through the tiny crack in the outside door.

What are Words?

Ideas and thoughts do not take distinct form until they are phrased in words. For *Helen Keller* (1880-1968), blind and deaf, the first thought to take form was W - A - T - E - R. It was pounded into her hand by *Anne Sullivan*, her illustrious teacher. Additional words came quickly after that defining moment, and her mind was liberated from its dark imprisonment. It was a startling revelation for her to discover that a particular word or words described a specific substance or an idea generally *for all time*. She revelled in the new world of words, and by imitation or origination she was radiant with -

> Now melts the snow; the warm winds blow; the waters flow.
> And robin dear is come to show that spring is here.

Words and language have an interesting history. "It is probable that language, as well as the faculty of speech, was the immediate gift of God in Eden" (*Noah Webster*, 1857).

"Language marks the beginning of a new era when the child is able to move from a primitive system of thought (picture thinking) to a higher mode of thought in which the word symbols predominate" (*Selma H. Fraiberg*, professor of Child Psychoanalysis, University of California School of Medicine). Words become a language which opens the door to knowledge.

Along the shores of Galilee, Jesus fed the thousands and then endeavored to instruct them that He was the "bread of life" (Jn. 6:1-35). Those who were too perplexed "walked with Him no more," whereupon Jesus said to the twelve, "Do you also want to go away?" It was at this point that Peter made that solid observation, "To whom shall we go? You have the *words* of eternal life" (Jn. 6:66-68).

"Words!"

> God wove a web of loveliness, of clouds and stars and birds,
> But made not anything at all so beautiful as words.
> —Anna H. Branch

Knowledge of letters and words is one of the greatest blessings that ever God bestowed on the children of men.

The Lord had already declared that "the words that I speak to you, are spirit, and they are life" (Jn. 6:63). The words of God are distinctive; they possess a very special property. God's words are immeasurably superior to all the words of men. Look at those "words," examine those "words" carefully: They are *pure*; they are *perfect*; they are *sure*; they are *true*; they are *right*; they are *sweet*; they are *incorruptible*; they are *enduring*; they are *great*; they are *precious*; they are *living*; they are *powerful*; they are *settled*; they are *holy* and they are *wonderful* (Ps. 19:7-10; 1 Pet. 1:23-25; 2 Pet. 1:4; Heb. 4:12; Ps. 119:89; Rom. 1:2; Ps. 119:129). Such "words" can come only "from the mouth of the Lord" and without them no one can "live" (Deut. 8:3).

God's testimonies, God's words were "founded" in the counsels of eternity (Ps. 119:152). God grounded them, established them and gave them their meaning and function. The words of God have their origin in God. He Himself initiated them. They are God-breathed, God-given and God-determined (2 Tim. 3:15, 16).

Let us always be fully convinced that these "words" are truly *God's words*—that they come from God and that they speak for God, and let such a conviction become transmitted to our children.

Instruction in Bible "words" should commence with infancy. *Rachel Masten* in west Texas learned the English alphabet and all the verses in the ABC book by the time she was just twenty-one months old, because her mother read the verses to her faithfully almost from the day of the child's birth.

A friend, visiting a young mother, found her sitting in a rocking chair holding her baby and a Bible. The friend said, somewhat humorously, "Are you reading to your baby?" "Yes," the young mother replied. "But do you think he understands?" "I am sure he does not understand now," continued the mother, "but I want his earliest memories to be that of hearing God's Word."

That mother had it right. This word we need to hear from the earliest of life to the last of life.

> "Sing them over again to me, wonderful words of life;
> Let me more of their beauty see, wonderful words of life."

Profound Little Questions

In committing God's Word to memory, the child begins to ponder the eternal, the invisible. Eternal things arouse curiosity and evoke questions such as Solomon himself could not have answered: Who made God? Did you ever see God? Who put the chick in the egg? Where did God get the soil and the seed? Where is God? Does God sleep? How many years in eternity? How far is it to heaven? Heaven becomes a place no less real than "Greenville" though it cannot be seen with these mortal eyes.

Anne Weatherholt tells about the five-year-old girl whose dog Fluffy died and shortly thereafter her grandfather. One day she told her mother, "God has given a car to Pappy and he is driving Fluffy around the clouds this very minute."

However incomplete our answers, let the "profound" questions never be evaded, and let there always be some substance in our answers—drawing always on some appropriate Scripture that might come to mind. The child's questions must always be regarded as the opening of a door for the light of truth.

In the end, the child's questions will find the most satisfactory answers in the words of God. At first the words have little meaning, and then understanding begins to come faintly. As *Helen M. Young* reminds us, "There is a time to point the way, to teach his heart to love God's Word, to love God's day, for children don't wait." With much repetition the Scriptures are stored in memory. Perseverance pays. Things that seem obscure today become plain tomorrow. Abstract things crystalize in the mind slowly. The child's concept of some superior power comes early. Invisible things begin to assume reality. The remembered "words of life" begin to form connections and, in time, the light of the gospel dawns upon the mind of the child.

When the Child Learns Scripture!

We plant the "incorruptible seed" in the mind of that infant. We water it with prayer day after day, month after month. In time, God's omnipotence enlightens and gives rise to a new life, generated by the Spirit and nourished by the Word that has been slowly assimilated. Then daily growth continues—"precept upon precept, line upon line, line upon line, here a little, there a little" until the tender heart perceives "the message," and with "stammering lips" utters "knowledge" (Isa. 28:9-11).

Jesus, Lord, I come to Thee, Thou hast said I may;
Tell me what my life should be, take my sins away.

Jesus, Lord, I learn of Thee, in Thy word divine;
Every promise there for me, may I call it mine.
— Frances Ridley Havergal

Remember Timothy? He was the apostle Paul's closest associate and he labored with him in the gospel "as a son with his father" (Phil. 2:22). This brings to mind the two little children who were trying to decide which was the last book of the Bible. Mary said that it was Timothy, but Frank, her brother, would not allow that. "No, Mary," he said, "the Bible does not end with Timothy but with REVOLUTION."

Though Timothy is not remembered as the last book of the Bible, the name has a far greater distinction, for it was of Timothy that the apostle said, "And that from a child you have known the Holy Scriptures, which are able to make you wise for salvation through faith which is in Christ Jesus" (2 Tim. 3:15).

The Greek word for "child" is *brephos*, and more precisely it means, "a babe, infant, babbler" in the very first months of life. Timothy was taking in the blessed word of God from the time of his infancy because of the firmly-founded faith of his mother Eunice and his grandmother Lois. They knew the value and the power of God's word; and they believed that when the word is engraved in the mind and heart it will provide a connection for the Holy Spirit to work supernatural "revolutions," beginning with "salvation." There is supernatural power in the Holy Scriptures. "Faith" finds its wisdom not in the thoughts of men, but in the thoughts of God in His Word.

No words of the "distinguished" Timothy are available, but he might easily have said, "It was not difficult for me to believe in Christ, the Messiah, because I had memorized Psalm 23 and Isaiah 53 as a young child. I could see that it was Jesus who is the 'Good Shepherd,' and that 'He was wounded for our transgressions.' I believed in Him with my whole heart. I could see how He was moving in the life of the apostle. We watched him being stoned at Lystra (2 Tim. 3:11). My mother applied ointment and bandaged his wounds in our home. I was constrained to go with the great apostle. My mother and grandmother encouraged me to do so."

Put the infant on the Word-bottle, keep the child in the Scriptures through grade school and middle school, and by the time he is in high school, he will very likely be doing it on his own, without parental authority or any outside constraints.

That child will never stop "eating" God's word. Like Jeremiah he will say, "Your words were found and I ate them" (15:16), or like Job who said, "I have treasured the words of His mouth more than my necessary food" (23:12).

Who can tell how early the minds of our children may gather the dew-drops of divine truth, and be made "wise for salvation." We do not press for early "decisions," as such, but we desire true regeneration and steady growth. For the "little ones," believing in the Savior is more simple and more complete by the very fact of their total helplessness. Dependency and trusting are almost instinctive especially with those who have caring parents. "I thank You, Father, Lord of heaven and earth, that You have hidden these things from the wise and prudent and have revealed them to babes" (Matt. 11:25).

The Bible Forget-Me-Nots

In our effort to encourage you in this great endeavor, we desire not only to arouse interest but also to provide you with materials to help accomplish this vital task. In this memory book there are ten special Bible verses which are to be implanted in the heart of your "special" child.

By two years of age "most children have vocabularies of about 270 words, and this increases to 2,600 words at the age of six" (Encarta 98 Enc.). There are 137 words in the ten Bible verses—half of the vocabulary of a two-year-old!

Each verse in this unique book begins with a verb, and children generally delight in verbs because they are action-words—beginning with that inviting, inducing word, "C-O-M-E," which took on singular and memorable meaning when the Lord spoke it in the presence of the small children who were brought to the Savior if only for a simple "touch" (Lu. 18:15,16).

As you teach the words to the child, draw repeated attention to the pictorial illustrations in the book, remembering the good counsel in the significant lines of *Horace*:

"Sounds which address the ear are lost and die in one short hour; but that which strikes the eye
Lives long upon the mind; the faithful sight engraves the knowledge with a beam of light."

Some recent studies show that a child remembers ten percent of what he hears, twenty-five percent of what he hears and sees, and ninety percent of what he hears, sees and practices.

Read to the child the "Little Lights" which come with the verse. The child will be looking at the color illustrations. Your purpose will be to engrave that Bible text in the mind of the child. You will want to study the fuller "illuminations" on each verse at the back of this book.

There are many enticing things out there in the world designed to capture the attention of that child. As the child takes to heart the message of the Scriptures, he will begin to recognize the disparity between worldly "success" and the true wealth of those who delight in God's Word "day and night" and who are "like a tree planted by the rivers of water, that brings forth its fruit in its season, whose leaf also shall not wither; and whatever he does shall prosper" (Ps. 1:3).

Reading the highlights of what happened in 1927, I came across *Yehudi Menuhin.* He was born in the United States of Russian parents. He began listening to music before he was two years old. At age three, he asked to learn how to play the violin. At age seven, he played with the San Francisco Symphony Orchestra. At age ten, he captivated the world in Paris as he played flawlessly "Symphonie Espagnole" (1927). Of Menuhin, who was paid $5,000 for a single concert, it was reported: "He seems to play his instrument almost as easily as a bird sings."

Riches and fame may be attained early, but as a Christian mother (or father), aspire rather to be a Bible *Jedidah* ("Beloved of the Lord") and your son will be a Bible *Josiah* ("Sustained of the Lord") who will be "humble," a "tender heart" who will enjoy the holy Scriptures and who will "perform the words" of the law all the days of his life (2 Kings 22:1 - 23:30).

Become excited about implanting God's Word in the mind and heart of your child. Let this be your passion, your calling, your *mantra.* The world has no particular interest in such things and has no yardstick by which to measure such achievements. Be but little impressed by the world— "its smiles and its scorning." Make it your aim, day after day, to have that little child memorize with such enthusiasm and with such perfection as to be able to speak God's Word as easily and as joyfully as "a bird sings."

Those Scriptures will help that child "grow in the grace and knowledge of our Lord" (2 Pet. 3:18), and will remind him to *continue* in the things he has learned (2 Tim. 3:14). The child will outgrow the ways of childhood, but he need never outgrow the habit of assimilating God's Word.

Little Lights with Forget-Me-Not 1

The disciples of Jesus told the mothers to take their little children away and not to bother their Master. But the loving Master said, please let the little children come to Me, and do not drive them away.

God make my life a little light,
Within the world to glow;
A tiny flame that burneth bright
Wherever I may go.
—M. Bentham-Edwards

— ⋆ —

"Tis Jesus loves the little ones
And He calls them as His own;
He's always with the little ones;
They are never left alone."

— ⋆ —

O dearest Book
Reflecting light from above,
We find in you the story of God's love.

— ⋆ —

As from the house your mother sees
You playing round the garden trees,
So you may see, if you will look
Through the windows of this book.
—R. L. Stevenson

1

But Jesus . . . said,
"Let the little children
come to Me,
and do not forbid them."

Luke 18:16

Little Lights with Forget-Me-Not 2

Long, long ago, a man who kept the jail was frightened and asked, "What must I do to be saved?" Paul and Silas, the missionaries who were put in jail answered, "Believe on the Lord Jesus Christ, and you will be saved."

I am trusting Thee, Lord Jesus,
Trusting only Thee;
Trusting Thee for full salvation,
Great, so great and free,
—Frances R. Havergal

— ✶ —

"Pure as the white, white snow,
Drifting in the vale below
You, Lord, can make me, I know,
Pure as the snow.
"Wash from my heart all sin;
Cleanse it from every stain;
Make me all pure within;
Pure as the snow."

— ✶ —

Jesus give the weary, calm and sweet repose;
With Thy tenderest blessing, may our eyelids close.
Grant to little children, visions bright of Thee;
So they won't be blinded by the things they see.
—Sabine Baring-Gould, altered

2

"Believe
on the Lord Jesus Christ,
and you will be saved."

Acts 16:31

Little Lights with Forget-Me-Not 3

When Samuel, in the Bible, was about three
years old, God called him by name, and Samuel
answered the way he was taught, Speak Lord,
Your servant hears You.

O give me Samuel's ear:
The open ear, O Lord,
Alive and quick to hear
Each whisper of Thy word!
Like him to answer at Thy call,
And to obey Thee first of all.
—James D. Burns

— ★ —

They say that God lives very high!
But if you look above the pines
You cannot see our God. And why?
But still I feel that His embrace
Slides down by thrills, through all things made,
Through sight and sound of every place.
—Elizabeth Barrett Browning

— ★ —

If my way is hard to choose,
Let me not Thy guidance lose.
If the path is very steep,
Lord, wilt Thou my footsteps keep?
—E. V.

3
"Speak, Lord,
for Your servant hears."
1 Samuel 3:9

Little Lights with Forget-Me-Not **4**

Here is a person asking God for help: Heal me Lord as only You can; save me from every problem, every sin, and then I will know for certain that I'm saved.

Little Max was dangerously ill. One day his mother came in the room and noticed the child's hand lying open as if to receive something. She asked him what it meant, and back came the answer in a whisper, "I can't think Mummy, what to pray, so I just put my hand there. God will see it, and He knows what I want."

— ✳ —

You are the *Way*, Lord! I follow You.
You are the *Truth*, Lord! I believe in You.
You are the *Life*, Lord! I am alive in You.

— ✳ —

"Today, tomorrow, forever, salvation is secure
For those whose trust is in Jesus,
His promises are sure."

— ✳ —

I saw the different things you did,
But always you yourself you hid,
I felt you push, I heard you call,
I could not see yourself at all—
O wind, a-blowing all day long,
O wind, that sings so loud a song!
—Robert Louis Stevenson

4

Heal me, O LORD,
and I shall be healed;
save me, and I shall be saved,
for You are my praise.

Jeremiah 17:14

Little Lights with Forget-Me-Not 5

Here is a prayer dressed up in very fine words: Protect me, Lord, as if I were the center of Your eye, and hide me under Your mighty wings.

Little Tim could go to sleep very easily, but each night he would wake screaming because he dreamed that he was falling down through space without any bottom to it. It was always a horror to him. This went on until his father showed him the verse in the fifth book of the Bible (33:27) - *"And underneath are the everlasting arms."* Tim now saw his safety and just *rested* on God's promise and slept soundly every night.

— ★ —

"Now the light has gone away;
Savior, listen while I pray,
Asking You to watch and keep
And to send me quiet sleep.

"Jesus, Savior, wash away
All that has been wrong today;
Help me every day to be
Good and gentle, more like Thee."

— ★ —

God watches o'er us all the day,
At home, at school, and at our play;
And when the sun has left the skies,
He watches with a million eyes.
—Gabriel Setoun

5

Keep me
as the apple of Your eye;
hide me under the shadow
of Your wings.

Psalm 17:8

Little Lights with Forget-Me-Not **6**

Teach me and lead me, O Lord,—teach me Your way, and guide me in a straight, level path because my enemies are out there.

God be in my head, and in my understanding;
God be in my eyes, and in my looking;
God be in my mouth, and in my speaking;
God be in my heart, and in my thinking;
God be in my living, and in my departing.

—Sarum Primer

— ✳ —

"Teach me how to trust Thee fully—
    How to go,
All my days in calm assurance,
    Since I know—
If I faithfully believe,
    All Thy blessing shall receive."

— ✳ —

My life is like a little book;
    A very little book indeed;
Here I'm writing my own story,
    And to God be praise and glory.

— ✳ —

Be like the bird, who
Halting in his flight on limb too slight
Feels it give way beneath him,
Yet sings, Knowing it has wings.

—Victor Hugo

6

Teach me Your way,
O LORD,
and lead me
in a smooth path.
Psalm 27:11

Little Lights with Forget-Me-Not 7

We are asked to taste, and see for ourselves that the Lord is good, and then we are told that the way to taste Him is to trust Him.

"Therefore, to you who believe, He is precious" (1 Pet. 2:7). The teacher asked the little children what the word "precious" meant. None could give an answer until it came to Stuart, the youngest, who said, very sweetly, "Mother is precious; we cannot do without her," and then hid his face in mother's apron.

— ＊ —

Some hae meat and canna eat,
   And some wad eat that want it;
But we hae meat and we can eat,
   And sae the Lord be thankit.
      —Robert Burns

— ＊ —

"Life is a very joyous thing,
Whatever we at times may say."

— ＊ —

I never saw a meadow, I never saw the sea;
   Yet know I how a flower looks,
     And what a wave must be.
I never spoke with God, nor visited in heaven;
   Yet certain am I of the spot
     As if the chart were given.
      —Emily Dickinson, altered

7

Oh, taste and see
that the LORD is good;
blessed is the man
who trusts in Him!

Psalm 34:8

Little Lights with Forget-Me-Not 8

We are taught in this verse to do things for the Lord with a glad and happy heart, and to come before Him with singing.

In the story of the ages
There are lines of tender grace,
Which our Father, in His purpose,
Let the little children trace:
Then, O Lord, may we be ready
To receive the call divine:
For we know our simple service
Is a part of Your design.
—W. H. Parker

— ★ —

I would be Jesus' helper, listening ev'ry day;
Doing as the Bible tells me in a cheerful way.
I would be Jesus' helper, serving Him each day;
Telling others, 'Jesus loves you,' in a happy way.

— ★ —

When young Jennilee sweeps a room
I vow she dances with the broom!
If ever you are full of gloom
Just watch Jennilee sweep a room!
—Nancy Byrd Turner

8

Serve the LORD
with gladness;
come before His presence
with singing.

Psalm 100:2

Little Lights with Forget-Me-Not 9

Here in this verse God asks all of us just to be still, to look around us, above us, and see all the wonderful things that He has made.

We thank You, dear God, for all lovely things;
For the pretty flowers and the little birds that sing;
For the butterflies, the green grass, and the trees;
For the big shining sun, twinkling stars, silver moon;
For sunset colors in the sky, and for the fleecy clouds;
We thank You, dear God, for all these lovely things.

—Edna Dean Baker

— ✱ —

Stand still a while, God's little ones,
   And see what God has made;
And listen to His holy word
   And learn how not to be afraid.

— ✱ —

Why is the sky?
What starts the thunder overhead?
   Who makes the crashing noise?
Are the angels falling out of bed?
   Are they breaking all their toys?
Does every star that happens to fall
   Turn into a fire-fly?
Can't it ever get back to Heaven at all?
   And why is the sky?

—Louis Untermeyer

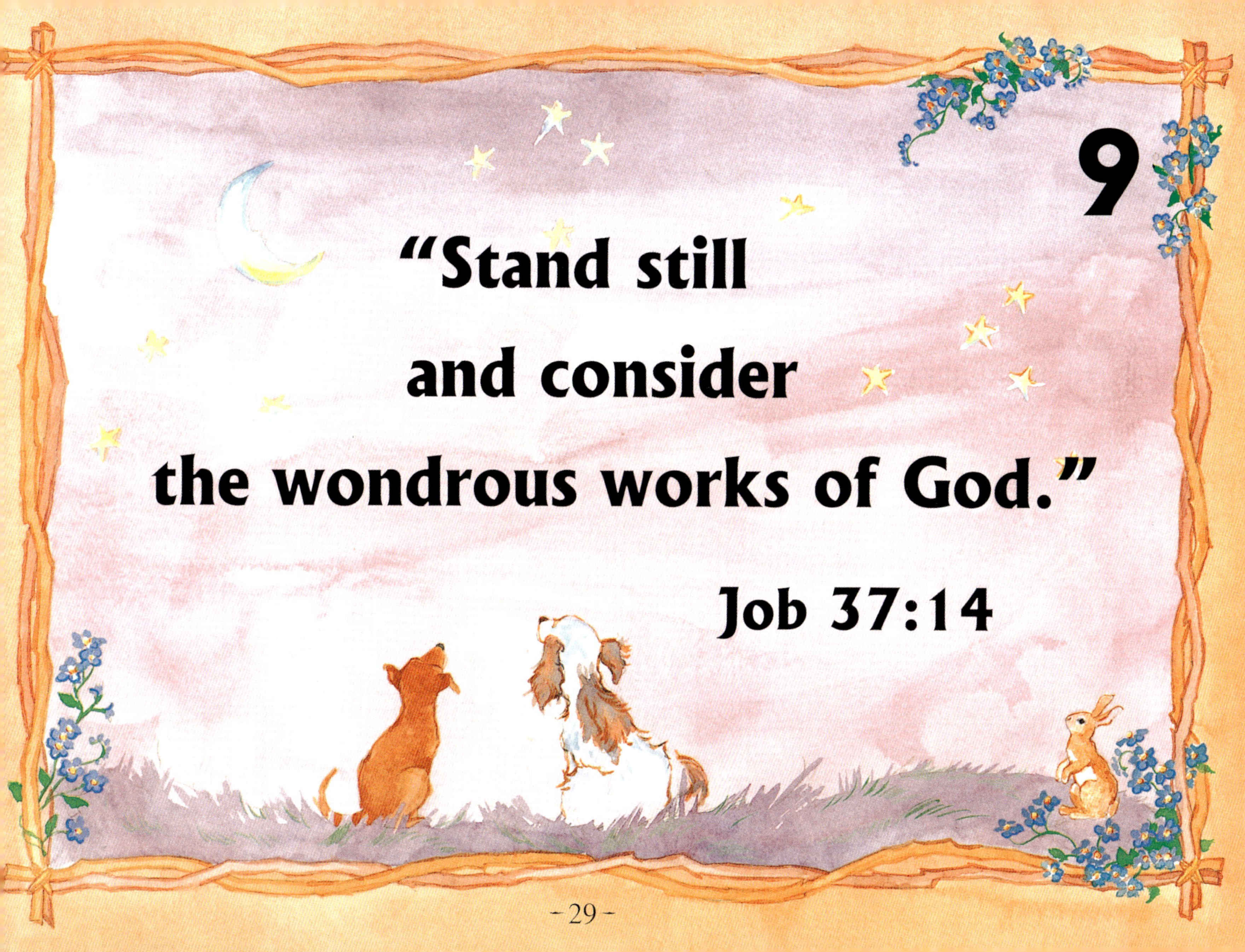
9
"Stand still
and consider
the wondrous works of God."
Job 37:14

Little Lights with Forget-Me-Not **10**

God is asking His children to place all their cares and problems on Him, and He assures them that He cares for them.

> Hush! my dear, lie still and slumber,
> Holy angels guard thy bed.
> Heavenly blessings without number
> Gently falling on thy head.
> —Isaac Watts

— ✱ —

> Robin Redbreast and sparrow Spot
> Visited together one spring morning.
> Said the robin to the sparrow,
> Friend, I'd really like to know
> Why the people rush around and worry so.
> At such a tho't, Spot began to cry,
> And said with a teeny sparrow sigh,
> I think it must surely be
> They don't have a kind, dear Father
> Such as cares for you and me.

— ✱ —

> "O Jesus, dost Thou love me,
> And dost Thou care for me?
> I scarcely dare to realize
> Such love, so great, so free!"

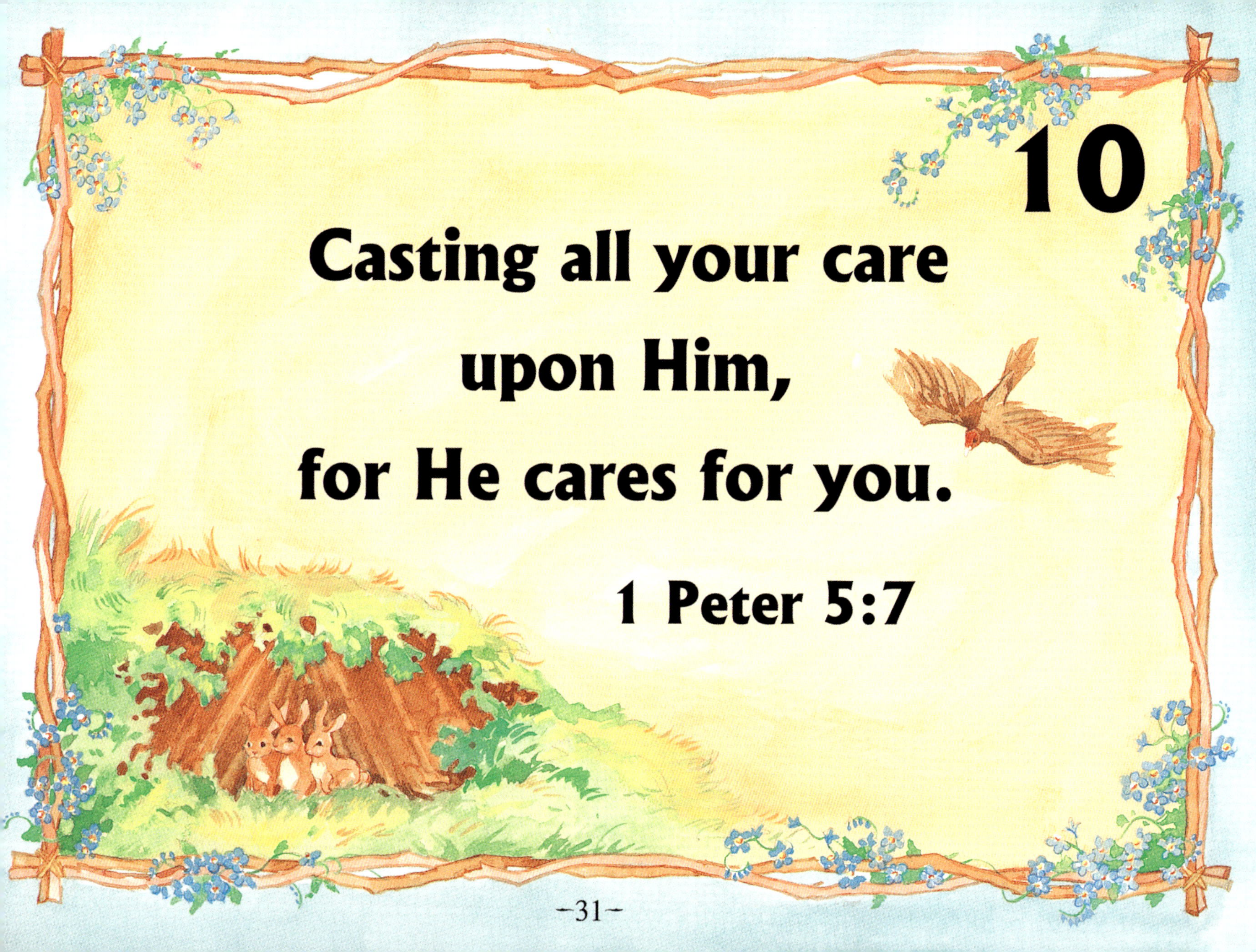
10
Casting all your care
upon Him,
for He cares for you.

1 Peter 5:7

Illuminations on the Ten Bible Verses

Here we have a fuller commentary on the ten verses in this Memory book. A few songs are included as well as other ideas. All this is to aid the parent or the teacher in explaining and applying the meaning of the verses to the child slowly—a little at a time. We want to implant that word in the mind of the little child in such a way that it will never be forgotten and will be a blessing all through life.

☆ Light on Luke 18:16 — Forget-Me-Not 1

But Jesus called them to Him and said, "Let the little children come to Me, and do not forbid them; for of such is the kingdom of God."

George Washington, the first president of the United States, loved children and enjoyed playing with them. One day he was invited out to dinner, and when the people gathered around the table, George Washington was missing. They found him upstairs playing with the children, and those children always remembered that special time.

Our text has the words of Jesus long ago when mothers brought their little children to Him, if only to "touch" them. The great apostles frowned on the idea and told the mothers to hush and to take those children away. It was then that Jesus quickly checked them by saying, "Let the little children come to Me, and do not forbid them."

We "forbid them," not so much by *disallowing*, but chiefly by *withholding*. "Withholding what?" By not showing those totally uninformed children the love of Jesus, the attitude of Jesus, the concern of Jesus—yes, the "words" of Jesus. To keep those helpless children in the dark in this way is to keep them from the outstretched arms of the Savior, who says ever so plainly, "Let the little children come to Me;" don't try to keep them away. Instead, tell them that "I am the door" to heaven, that "I am the good shepherd" who died for them and that "no one comes to the Father except through Me."

A child may learn in a Christian home to play, to pray, to speak and to act as in the presence of that special Playmate and Friend. The mystic poet Blake could not remember a time when the unseen Friend was not real to him. At four years of age, he declared that he saw God through a window. It seems God gives little children eyesight that comprehends the unseen. On the verse "Where two or three are gathered in my name, there am I in the midst"—the early Church Fathers considered the "two" to be the parents, and the third to be the little child, placed in such a home so as to become acquainted with the Lord early in life.

It was *Abraham Lincoln* who said on one occasion, "God makes a man's face, but a man makes his own countenance." In the life of the "little one" the face and the countenance are both alike.

> God sends us many a thing that purifies;
>   But none for power and beauty can excel
>   The guileless look in little children's eyes.
>   —Kennedy Williamson

The Story of Sarah Sinclair

Let me pass along a beautiful true story I read in a Christian magazine published in 1870. Little *Sarah Sinclair* was born in Edinburgh, Scotland in 1860. Her watchful mother "became satisfied that Sarah had been made a partaker of God's glorious grace when she was three; and the little hymn, which at the time was her favorite, seemed to indicate the dear child's own consciousness that a great era in her almost infant life had been reached:

> "I'm glad I ever saw the day,
>   Sing glory, glory, glory,
> When first I learn't to sing and pray
>   Of glory, glory, glory."

The entire story about this dear child is compelling. She lived only five and a half years. Sarah knew many Bible verses and hymns. She loved to pray and talk about the Lord with other children. She would recite the verses and hymns in praying and in talking with her brother Tommy and with other children. Two weeks before she went to "be with Jesus," Sarah, on a certain "Examination" day, recited a hymn before a large assembly. *Miss Haldane* lifted her gently, and placed her upon a pedestal. A hum could be heard across the room as the wee figure stood erect and in her "blessed unconsciousness" proceeded to recite one of her favorite hymns. She threw so much expression into the words and her effort to pronounce big words correctly was so beautiful. Here is the hymn she recited:

> "I am a very little child,
> I'm very young and very wild,
>   And sometimes naughty too.
> I'm led by many a foolish thought,
> To do the things I never ought
>   To think of or to do.

> "But God, the holy God above,
> Is very kind and full of love
>   For little ones like me,
> And He will hear me, if I pray;
> And He will teach me every day,
>   A better child to be.

> "Jesus, Thou know'st how weak I am:
> Oh! lead me like a little lamb,
>   And I will follow Thee.
> Take all my naughtiness away,
> And let me never go astray,
>   Until Thy face I see."

Keep the important question connected with the verse before the child day after day and help the child to give the answer.

Ten Little Children

Mary LeBar

From Old Tune
Arr. by Harry Dixon Loes

☆ Light on Acts 16:31 — Forget-Me-Not 2

So they said, "Believe on the Lord Jesus Christ, and you will be saved, you and your household."

Sir John Franklin (1786-1847), a British explorer, who surveyed the coast line of northern Canada, said when he was a young boy, "When I am big, I'm going to build a ladder so high that I shall be able to climb to heaven."

But no such ladder can be built. Jesus is the only way to heaven. He said, "I am the way, the truth and the life. No one comes to the Father except through Me" (Jn. 14:6).

Let us teach our little children the name of Jesus and help them to trust Him as Savior.

"Lord, I believe you died for me,
    There on the cross of Calvary
From all my sin to set me free, Lord I believe;
    Lord I believe You saved my soul,
Cleansed my poor heart and made me whole."

- - -

You ask how you learn to trust Him?
Dear child, you must just let go!

Let go of your frantic worry,
And the fears which plague you so;

Let go of each black tomorrow
Which you try to live today;

Let go of your fevered planning,
He knoweth all your way.

Fear not lest your slipping fingers
Let go of your Saviour too,

Trusting is only knowing
He'll not let go of you!
> —Martha Snell Nicholson

You may know a great deal *about* Christ but not be trusting Him and resting in Him for salvation.

David was on the roof of a high building where several men were at work. He was walking around with apparent unconcern when his foot slipped and he fell. In falling, he had enough presence of mind to lay hold of a rope at hand, and hung suspended in the air alongside of the building. At this fearful moment, Jack Stem, a big man on the ground below saw what was taking place; he extended his arms and called to the boy, "Let go of the rope and I will catch you; I can do it; let go and trust me." David hesitated a moment, and then realizing his danger, he let go of his hold on the rope and dropped safely into the arms of Jack Stem.

This illustrates the simple act of believing and of the immediate and complete deliverance. The boy saw his danger; he heard the voice, he believed the man, he let go of his rope dependency, and he dropped into the arms of his deliverer.

A little child of seven
> Or even three or four

Can enter into heaven
> Through Christ, the Open Door.

For when the heart believeth
> On Christ, the Son of God,
'Tis then the child receiveth
> Salvation through His blood.

On the Humorous Side

"What do you believe?" said George Whitefield (1714-1770), the English Evangelist, to a miner in Cornwall. "What the Church believes," was his reply. "And what does the Church believe?" "What I believe." "And what do you both believe?" again asked Whitefield. "The same thing," was the miner's reply.

> "What must I do to be saved?" is the biggest question in the world. And what is the answer?

One, Two, Three, Four . . .

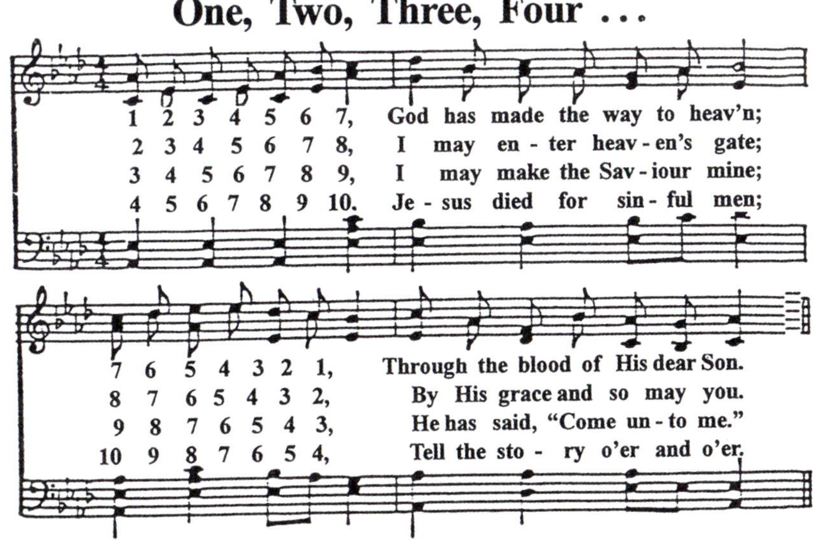

☆ **Light on 1 Sam. 3:9—Forget-Me-Not 3**

Therefore Eli said to Samuel, "Go lie down; and it shall be, if He calls you, that you must say, 'Speak, Lord, for your servant hears.'"

Here, we have one of the most remarkable stories in the Bible, and this was a new beginning for God's ancient people, Israel.

In those days, the word of God was very rare, and they did not have a true spokesman for God (1 Sam. 3:1). Eli, the priest at God's house was old, and his two sons were very evil. Hannah, a true believer, prayed for a son. God answered her prayer and a son was born whom she named "Samuel." The name Samuel means "asked of the Lord" (1 Sam. 1:20).

When Samuel was "weaned," (1 Sam. 1:24), about three years old, as the Hebrews tell us, she presented him to Eli at the house of the Lord, and said, "Therefore I also have lent him to the Lord; as long as he lives he shall be lent to the Lord" (1 Sam. 1:28). Observe, the words "lent to the Lord" are very close to the same meaning as "asked of the Lord."

Each year, Hannah made Samuel a new little linen coat which was called an "ephod," and Samuel probably had something to give his loving mother when she came.

Although at this time Samuel "did not yet know the Lord" (1 Sam. 3:7), yet three times, we are told, that "he ministered to the Lord before Eli" (1 Sam. 2). He could light a candle, hold a dish, run an errand, shut the door, and *this* is "ministry." Three times God called "Samuel" and then Eli told Samuel *how* to answer (as we should tell our children). "Now the Lord came and stood and called as at other times, 'Samuel! Samuel!' and Samuel answered, [softly, and perhaps with a pause of wonder and awe] 'Speak, for Your servant hears'" (1 Sam. 3:4-10).

The next day the young "prophet," whom God had called, took care of his simple duty— "opened the doors of the house of the Lord"—and told Eli "everything."

God's old servant understood, and said quietly, *It is the Lord*" (Sam. 3:10-18).

Day by day, dear Lord of Thee
Three things I pray:
 To see Thee more clearly,
 To love Thee more dearly,
 To follow Thee more nearly,
  Day by day.
  —St. Richard of Chichester

A minister's wife was starting out for a walk, and invited her little daughter to go with her. "No, mamma, I can't" was the very positive reply. "Why not?" "I have to help papa." "Help papa! In what way?" "Why, he told me to sit here in this corner and keep quiet and help him write his sermon, and I don't believe he is half done yet."

> **How old must a person be in order to be a "servant" of God?**

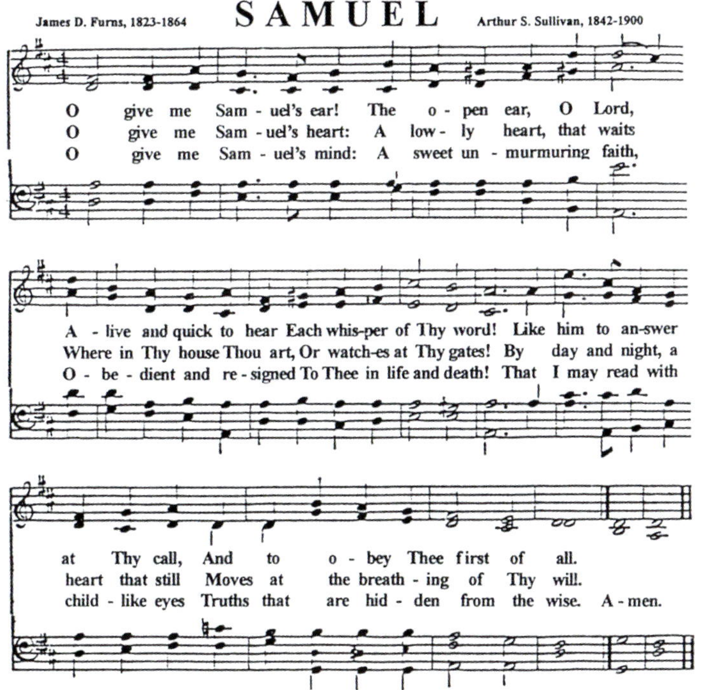

☆ Light on Jer. 17:14 — Forget-Me-Not 4

Heal me, O LORD, and I shall be healed; Save me, and I shall be saved, for You are my praise.

It is very illuminating just to close your eyes and repeat the words of this verse four or six times, and ponder the meaning of what He did, and speedily there will appear the portrait of the Good Shepherd outstretched on that cruel tree (Jn. 10:11); or the picture in Peter's house where "his wife's mother [was] lying sick with a fever. So He touched her hand, and the fever left her" (Matt. 8:14, 15).

> He touched her hand and the fever left her;
> He touched her hand as He only can;
> With the wondrous skill of the great Physician,
> With the tender touch of the Son of Man.

Touch is that "faculty" which love employs and the power with which God delivers.

It was a very dark night when betrayal and conspiracy surrounded our Lord in Gethsemane. When the disciples saw what was about to happen, "they said to Him, 'Lord, shall we strike with the sword?'" (Lu. 22:49). Peter at once came to the defense of the Lord, even as he had promised, and with over-heated machinery in his soul, drew his sword, and slashed off the right ear of Malchus, the intruding slave servant of that cunning Caiaphas (Jn. 18:10).

Here it was that the Lord, clothed with the majesty of Omnipotence, intervened, "Put your sword into the sheath," He said to Peter, (Jn. 18:11), and turning to the wounded one, "He touched his ear and healed him," (Lu. 22:51), and we like to think that, in that healing moment, He delivered him also from the penalty and slavery of sin, for salvation of the eternal soul is far greater than the healing of the fragile body.

Like little children, let us all be "living in touch" with the Healer of body and soul!

We must also remember that the Lord can heal simply by speaking the word. The centurion's servant was sick and he said to Jesus, "Only speak a word, and my servant will be healed." Jesus marveled at his faith and said, "Go your way; and as you have believed, so let it be done for you" (Matt. 8:6-13).

In Psalm 107, we read: "Then they cried out to the Lord in their trouble . . . He sent His word and healed them, and delivered them from their destructions" (19, 20).

On the Humorous Side

A story is told about a niece of Bishop Phillips Brooks. The child was three years old. Her mother was preparing her for bed, when she had a call down stairs; as she was about to leave the room, she said: "Dear, say your prayers while mamma is gone." When she returned she asked the child if she had said her prayers. The little one replied: "I did and I didn't." "Why, what do you mean, dear?" asked the mother. "I told the Lord I was very tired, and couldn't say my prayers; and He said, 'Don't mention it, Miss Brooks.'"

☆ Light on Psalm 17:8 — Forget-Me-Not 5

Keep me as the apple of Your eye; hide me under the shadow of Your wings.

In this verse we learn how David, long ago, asked God to keep him and protect him. He says "keep me as the apple of Your eye." What is the apple of the eye? It is that little round black spot in the very center which we call the "pupil." Of all the parts of the eye that can be seen, the pupil is the most important, because it is through the pupil that the light enters, and if anything happens to injure it seriously, the person becomes blind.

Now the eye is a very delicate instrument, and can be very easily hurt, but God has set up about the eye carefully designed defenses. The *eyebrows* are guards number one; they keep the sweat from running down into the eyes. The second guards are the *eyelashes*; they act like fine-hair brushes to sweep away specks of dust that might hurt. Then there are the heavy guards, the *eyelids*, like big sliding doors, which come down swiftly at the approach of any danger.

The eyeball rests on a soft bed of fat on which it can move with ease and is protected by a surrounding bone socket. Then every time the eye winks, a tear from the tear-gland falls and washes the surface of the eyeball.

How marvelously and completely the "apple of the eye" is protected! So, along with David, we must ask God to *keep* us in His own wonderful ways—keep us from temptations, from evil and from all dangers by day and by night.

And if you were to ask Ginny, the chick, where was the best place to hide from danger, Ginny would tell that it is right there under the wings of mother-hen. So *we* always run for cover under God's wings.

God is always near me, hearing what I say;
  Knowing all my thoughts and deeds, all my work and play.

God is always near me, in the darkest night;
  He can see me just the same as by mid-day light.

God is always near me, though so young and small;
  Not a look or word or thought, but God knows it all.
                                              —Philip P. Bliss

On the Humorous Side

Little Nelly was five years old. Her mother had taken great pains to instill into her mind principles of right and truth.

One day she stood at the door of the dining room, looking with great earnestness at a basket of fine peaches which was on the table. Nelly knew she should not touch them without leave, but the temptation was strong. Soon her mother, who was watching her from another room, saw her bow her head and cover her face with her little hands. "What ails you, Nelly?" she said. The child, startled, not knowing she was watched, "Oh, mother," she exclaimed, "I wanted so much to take one of the peaches; but *first* I thought I would ask God if He had any objection."

Who is best able to protect the child of God? Why?

"Take this child and nurse it for me"—
  So King Pharaoh's daughter spake
To the mother, whose whole being
  For her little one did ache.

So God speaks to every mother
  At her helpless infant's birth:
"Take this child and nurse it for Me
  In all its early years on earth."
                                              —Author unknown

☆ Light on Psalm 27:11—Forget-Me-Not 6

Teach me Your way, O LORD, and lead me in a smooth path, because of my enemies.

Allie, when but a wee little girl, sat down on the green sofa, with a big book upside-down in her lap, and called, "Mother dear, please come here and teach me." Michael, also, still

quite small, put his little feet on the keys of the smart computer and said with much earnestness, "Daddy, could you come and show me how."

> Ere your boy has reached to seven,
>   Teach him well the way to heaven;
> Better still the lad will thrive,
>   If he learns before he's five.

Straighten the trees when they are little saplings, and train children when they are very young. Begin early to teach because children begin early to sin. "Train up a child in the way he should go, and when he is old he will not depart from it" (Prov. 22:6). What is learned early is learned for life. Persist in teaching them complete obedience without bearing down too tightly. People are all born blind on the inside and do not understand the things about God until He teaches them inwardly. God gives us big ears on the inside when we ask Him. David in one Psalm (119) asks God at least nine times, "teach me." And Job said, "Teach me *what* I do not see" (34:32). God gives us the kind of eyesight that sees the unseen. "Teach me, and I will hold my tongue; cause me to understand wherein I have erred" (Job 6:24).

"If transistors can snatch up songs from out of the air for us to hear . . . If TV screens can bring us news at once from far and near . . . Shouldn't we trust Almighty God to hear what we say when we pray?" (*Margaret J. Anderson*).

When the great French painter, *Jean Francois Millet* (1815-75 - "The Angelus," "The Reapers") was but a little fellow, he and his father stood on the cliffs one evening to watch the sunset. The wonderful crimson of the sky and the golden glory of the sea made Francois cry out with delight, but his father stood still, took off his cap, and said with quiet awe, "My son . . . *it is God*" (Ps. 19:1).

On the Serious Side

"What seems to be the trouble?" mamma asked.

"Why," explained Johnnie, as soon as he could speak, "we each had two pieces of cake, and there was only one left, and Jennie took it—she took it all."

Mamma looked perplexed, and said, "That does seem rather selfish of Jennie!"

"Yes, it was!" Johnnie wept, " 'cause I cut the cake that way so's I could have the extra piece myself."

☆ Light on Psalm 34:8 — Forget-Me-Not 7

Oh, taste and see that the LORD is good; blessed is the man who trusts in Him!

"How can I know if the Lord is good?" a child inquired. "Son," his mother said, "how do you know if you have sugar in your tea?" The soul of a person has its "senses" as well as the body. "O taste and see."

There is a kind of *jubilation* of believers in Psalm 34. One man confesses that he had been hounded by relentless fears, "I sought the Lord, and He heard me, and delivered me from all my fears." Then a small group of cheerful witnesses testified that in past days their faces had been clouded with sorrow, because the "sunshine" of heaven had gone out of their souls: "They looked to Him and were radiant, and their faces were not ashamed."

Then another person bore clear witness that he had been in many tight places, surrounded by many temptations and the Lord delivered him from their destructions: "This poor man cried out, and the Lord heard him, and saved him out of all his troubles." Then they seemed to merge into one chorus of joyful assurance: "The angel of the Lord encamps all around those who fear Him."

And from these united testimonies, there comes this mighty invitation, "*Oh taste and see that the Lord is good.*"

"All that thrills my soul is Jesus;
He is more than life to me."

But there are so many people—young and older—around us who have never *tasted* the goodness of the Lord, and they can do that first by trusting Him, for this is what we find in the text: "blessed is the man who trusts in Him." Trusting in Jesus as Savior is the very same thing as believing in Him as Savior.

To trust Christ requires only to rest completely in the finished work of Christ, and the blessedness of full assurance will flood the mind and soul of the believing one, and the "taste" of his incomparable goodnesses will surely follow.

"Bless the Lord, O my soul; and all that is within me, bless His holy name! Bless the Lord, O my soul, and forget not all His benefits: Who forgives all your iniquities, Who heals all your diseases, Who redeems your life from destruction, Who crowns you with lovingkindness and tender mercies, Who satisfies your mouth with good things, so that your youth is renewed like the eagle's."

There is an interesting story about the great poet, Alfred Tennyson (1809-92). When together with a friend in a garden, he was asked, what he thought of Jesus Christ. Tennyson walked in silence until they came to a sunflower, with its fine bloom lifted always to the sun. Pointing to it, he said, "What the sun is to that flower, Jesus Christ is to my soul. He is the sun of my soul."

On the Serious Side

Alick was only ten years old and he worked every day as a "chimney sweep" many years ago.

A friend once asked him, "Do you ever pray?" "Oh, yes! sir."

"And when do you do it? You go out very early in the morning, do you not?" "Yes, sir," the boy replied, "and I am only half awake when I leave the house. I think about God, but cannot say that I pray then." "So, when do you pray?" the friend asked.

"Well, sir, our master orders us to mount the chimney quickly, but does not forbid us to rest a little when we reach the top. Then I sit on the chimney and pray."

"And what do you say in your prayer, Alick?"

"Ah, sir, very little. I know not any grand words with which to speak to God. Most frequently, I repeat two verses that I learned at school." When asked what they were, Alick recited them fervently, "The Lord is good to all, and His tender mercies are over all His works," and, "God be merciful to me a sinner."

☆Light on Psalm 100:2 — Forget-Me-Not **8**

Serve the LORD with gladness; come before His presence with singing.

When we go to a restaurant, we much prefer the waitress who serves with a cheerful spirit.

Patricia St. John, an English missionary, remembers when she was about two, she was found in her baby bed holding the rail, bouncing up and down with considerable merriment and making quite a noise. When asked by her mother what she thought she was doing, her reply was sure and Scriptural, "I'se always 'bounding in de work of de Lord."

A small boy named Tommy said once to his mother, "I wish Jesus lived on earth now."

"Why," asked his mother. "Because," he said, "I would like to be doing something for Him."

"But what could a boy like you do?" asked his mother. "I could run errands for Him," Tommy answered.

"So you could; well, then, take this glass of jelly over to Madison, the girl across the street who is so good to you."

Each child of God can be a *mind* through which Christ thinks, a *heart*, through which Christ loves, a *voice* through which Christ speaks, a *hand* through which Christ serves, two *feet* through which Christ walks, a cheerful *person* in whom Christ lives.

Mrs. Gloria Bonar, was a widow in Scotland, who had reared four boys with Bible names—Matthew, Mark, Luke and John. One day her pastor came upon her in the kitchen where she stood weeping. When asked what was the matter, she easily confessed, "I am so miserable and unhappy; from the time I was a little girl, I have always wanted to do something for Jesus."

"Well, haven't you?" asked the minister.

"I will tell you," she said in her humble confession, "all I've done is wash dishes, cook three meals a day, take care of the children, mopped the floor and mended clothes—that's all I have done all my life, and I always wanted to do something for Jesus."

The pastor, sat back in the arm chair, looked at her and smiled, and asked about the boys. "Oh, my boys!"

And here was the outreach of her humble service: Matthew and Mark were missionaries in China. Luke was a missionary in Africa where a revival had broken out, and John her "baby," now nineteen, had just informed his mother that God had called him to go to Africa and help his brother, and "I'm so happy about that," she said.

The pastor then looked at her: "And you say that your life has been wasted in trivial tasks. I'd like to have your mansion when you are called Home."

"Spin cheerfully, not tearfully, though wearily you plod; spin carefully, spin prayerfully, but leave the thread with God."

On the Serious Side

"Rose, dear," the faithful mother said, "don't forget to pray in all the hurry of the morning." "No, mamma," the happy little girl replied, "I think of praying as part of my getting dressed."

"Listen to this, O Job; stand still and consider the wondrous works of God."

"Stand still!" Sometimes that's the hardest thing to do, especially for the little ones, for they must always be wiggling and doing things. We must ask the Lord to help us to be still.

We are asked to "stand still" in order that we might "consider" the wonders of God above us and all around us.

William G. Moorehead (1836-1914) in Ohio, would occasionally spin a fable, like that about the bird and a mole.

The bird was sitting on a branch of a tree and singing with all his heart. The little mole buried in the ground heard him and called out, "O bird, why are you making such a noise?"

The bird replied, "O Mr. Mole, the sun is so beautiful and everything around me is so lovely that I cannot help but sing."

The mole answered, "Why, Mr. Bird, I don't see anything beautiful in this world. I see only roots, and fishworms."

"Well, Mr. Mole, if you'd come out into the sunlight you'd find that you just had to sing."

David the Psalmist, delighted to see how "the heavens declare the glory of God . . . day unto day utters speech, and night unto night reveals knowledge" (Ps. 19:1, 2). The glories of the day are dissolved into the glories of the night as if shifted by the unseen hands of the mighty angels. Like the Psalmist, we are greatly impressed when we look in the sky and see the sun, the moon and all the stars, and then think that Jesus—the Son of God—would visit our tiny world and teach us so much about life and about heaven (Ps. 8:3, 4).

The sun is ninety-three million miles away and is many times larger than the earth. The sun gives light, heat and power, and it makes every flower, every plant and every tree grow, blossom and bear fruit.

The moon is much closer—only 240,000 miles away, and its light is borrowed from the sun.

> Great is the sun, and wide he goes
>   Through empty heaven without repose;
> And in the blue and glowing days
>   More thick than rain he showers his rays.
>
> Above the hills, along the blue,
>   Round the bright air with footing true.
> To please the child, to paint the rose,
>   The gardener of the world, he goes.
>   —R. L. Stevenson

There are many more stars than we can count, and the stronger the telescopes, the more stars appear. Some astronomers think that there are stars out there so far away that their light has not yet reached the earth. The stars are too far away to be measured with miles, so the distance is measured by light years, and yet the Bible tells us that God "counts the number of the stars; He calls them all by name" (Ps. 147:4).

I am a little child, and I am ignorant and weak; I gaze into the starry sky, and then I cannot speak. For all behind the starry sky, behind the world so broad, behind men's hearts, and souls doth lie the infinit-e of God.

—George Macdonald

What is the greatest thing that God has done for you?

THE WONDER SONG

GRACE W. OWENS   CLARA LEE PARKER

☆ Light on 1 Peter 5:7— Forget-Me-Not 10

Casting all your care upon Him, for He cares for you.

Most Christians seem willing enough to bring to God a little here and there of their sorrows and burdens, but the invitation in this text teaches us to cast "all" our cares upon Him, with the complete assurance that He does indeed "care" for us.

Worry and prayer fight each other, an old commentator said, like fire and water! Why worry and fret when you can pray and trust the Lord?

"I'm only a little sparrow, a bird of low degree:
My life is of little value but the dear Lord cares for me.
He gives me a coat of feathers—it's very plain, I know:
Without a speck of crimson, for 'twas not made for show."

Teach me a love of little things: teach my blind heart to see, that Thou who carest for little things art the God who cares for me.

Take your burden to the Lord and *leave* it there. "Cast your burden on the Lord, and He shall sustain you" (Ps. 55:22).

Who will take care of me? darling, you say!
  Lovingly, tenderly watched as you are!
Listen! I give you the answer today.
  One who is never forgetful or far.

He will take care of you! all through the year,
  Crowning each day with His kindness and love,
Sending you blessing and shielding from fear,
  Leading you on to that City above.
                    —Frances Ridley Havergal

You can never get beyond God's care, for it is always reaching you; you can never be outside of it, for it is always enfolding you.

Corrie ten Boom says that she learned of "my heavenly Father's love and care through my own father. When I was afraid and couldn't sleep, he would put his big hand over my little face." When she was in prison under the Nazis, she would say to the Lord, "Father, just put Your big hand over my little face. Then I could sleep."

On the Serious Side

You twitter and twitter,
  Yet this is not all
God knows every motion;
  He knows when you fall.

Little bird, little bird,
  Singing there in the tree,
I wish others also knew,
  What you are singing to me.
                    —Jennie M. Drinkwater

Father, lead me day by day,
Ever in Thine own sweet way;
Teach me to be pure and true,
Show me what I ought to do.

When I'm tempted to do wrong,
Make me steadfast, wise and strong;
And when all alone I stand,
Shield me with Thy mighty hand.

When my heart is full of glee,
Help me to remember Thee;
Happy most of all to know
That my Father loves me so.
                    —John Page Hopps

The Teacher Trembles

Noble Halliburton, Tennessee, remembers when his little son, Alfred, said to him one day, "Papa, if I do all you tell me to do, will God love me and take me to heaven?"

When confronted with such enormous questions from the little ones, the parents and teachers tremble.

Leslie P. Hill reflected on that responsibility with great concern:

Lord, who am I to teach the way
To little children day by day,
So prone myself to go astray?

I teach them knowledge, but I know
How faint they flicker, and how low
The candles of my knowledge glow.

I teach them power to will and do,
But only now to learn anew
My own great weakness through and through.

I teach them love for all mankind
And all God's creatures, but I find
My love comes lagging far behind.

Lord, if their guide I still must be,
O let the little children see
The teacher leaning hard on Thee.

The teacher must always remember that Jesus is the "way" to heaven. There is no other way. (Jn.14:6).

"God bless you, my dear child,
And keep you safe from harm,
And pillow soft your tender head
On Jesus' loving arm.

"We leave you safe with Him who says,
'Suffer the children dear
To come to Me, forbid them not,
No danger need they fear.'

"Oh! may your heart be early open
To Christ, the children's friend,
And may your life be spent for Him,
Until for you He does send.

"God bless you, darling little one,
And keep you pure, sweet love,
Until you reach your Home at last,
Within His fold above."

When an Infant Held the Attention of the World

On October 14, 1987, in Midland, Texas, Jessica McClure, eighteen months old, fell into an abandoned water well, eight inches wide, and wedged to a stop 22 feet down, one leg stuck straight above her tiny shoulders in the rocky chute.

Within hours of her fall, people around the world, including the U. S. President, were following the story with incredible interest via radio and television. The child's survival in that precarious position seemed to hang as by a thread. Christians prayed for her deliverance.

The Amazing Rescue

Mining and drilling experts joined hands with the local rescue workers. Huge highway construction equipment and jackhammers were brought on the scene and began to bore and blast a deep hole, five feet from the well. This continued day and night for more than forty-eight hours. On October 16, Jessica was raised from her deep grave bruised and bleeding, but alive.

The Unreported Drama

For fifty-eight hours baby Jessica had remained isolated in that frightful dark hole. Outside of a few whimpers, she occupied "herself by singing nursery rhymes." Surely an unseen Visitor was with her. Was it a special angel or was it the Lord Himself who so miraculously upheld her?—comforting her and

From a mural at Midland, Texas, "Triumph of Human Spirit."
Photo: The Dallas Morning News/Doug Holt, Used by permission.

giving strength to her little body in that painful position, and instead of screaming, she was "singing."

Father, I cannot see Thy face,
    Though mine is turned to Thee
And yet I feel Thee *very near*;
    I know Thou *seest me*.